Surviving the Terrible Teenage Years

DR. CLIFF SCHIMMELS

LIFEJOURNEY
BOOKS

LifeJourney Books is an imprint of David C. Cook
Publishing Co.
David C. Cook Publishing Co., Elgin, Illinois 60120
David C. Cook Publishing Co., Weston, Ontario
Nova Distribution, Ltd., Torquay, England

Surviving the Terrible Teenage Years
©1991 by Cliff Schimmels
(This booklet consists of selected portions of *What
Parents Try to Forget About Adolescence* ©1989 by Cliff
Schimmels)

Edited by Brian Reck
Cover design by Bob Fuller
First printing, 1991
Printed in the United States of America
95 94 93 92 91 5 4 3 2 1

Library of Congress Cataloging in Publication Data
Schimmels, Cliff
Surviving the Terrible Teenage Years
Cliff Schimmels
   p. cm. — (Helping Families Grow series)
ISBN: 1-55513-662-1
1. Parent and teenager—United States. 2. Junior High
students—United States—Social conditions. 3. Parenting
—Religious aspects—Christianity.   I. Title.   II. Series:
HQ799.15S35 1991
649'.125—dc20   91-26512
                                                    CIP

Chad and Kenneth were on the seventh-grade basketball team together. Kenneth was one of the most responsible thirteen-year-olds I have ever known. He was always the first one to practice, but that is understandable because he kept his locker neat and orderly. He didn't have to hunt for his shoes or report one of his socks stolen (when he had really lost it). He took care of his equipment. He was always the first one out to practice.

Once on the practice floor, Kenneth did everything the coach asked. When the players ran laps, he always ran next to the wall and didn't cheat on the corners, even when the coach wasn't looking. When the coach blew his whistle, Kenneth immediately stopped dribbling and ran in to hear what the coach had to say. Kenneth bought a stocking cap because Coach said to cover his head after practice. When Coach said to shoot with the left hand, Kenneth worked on it at home until he could do it. Not only did Kenneth know his own position, he also knew where every other player was supposed to be at all times. In short, Kenneth was a very responsible person and player.

On the other hand, one might have gotten the idea that Chad didn't care. He was late to practice almost every day, and he even skipped some times. Actually, he often had a good excuse because his teachers had kept him after school, but he still missed practice. His locker was a shambles. His socks never matched. When lap time came, Chad loafed and cut corners. When Coach blew his whistle, Chad always took time to shoot another basket before he came in. He never listened when Coach talked—it was evident by the way he played. Chad never knew where he was supposed to be, so the coach had to hold up practice just to show him the correct position. In short, Chad was a very irresponsible person and player.

But I forgot to mention that Kenneth

was four-six while Chad was an even six feet tall and well-developed for his age.

As the day of the first game approached, Kenneth became excited. A couple of days before, the coach had handed out uniforms. They might have looked like old eighth-grade hand-me-downs to you, but to Kenneth they were on par with what the Chicago Bulls wear. He didn't mind that he was the last person to get a uniform—at least he had one. After his mother tucked it in for him a bit, he hung it on his door so he could look at it and dream.

On the day of the game, Kenneth was the first one into the dressing room. He dressed quickly and waited for Coach to come and give that powerful speech before they went out on the floor. But when the coach got there, what he saw first was Chad—leaning against his locker, still in street clothes. Chad had forgotten his uniform.

Coach ranted and raved and talked of responsibility, while Chad hung his head and grinned. Finally, Coach devised a plan. Chad would just have to wear Kenneth's uniform, even if it looked ridiculous on him. Kenneth could sit on the bench and keep shot charts.

"Fiend!" you shout. "Foul! What a horrible man. How could he do such a despicable thing?"

But I ask you, if you were a young coach trying to win at the seventh-grade level in the hope of moving up to high school coaching, would you have let a six-foot giant sit on the bench on the small technicality that he had forgotten his uniform—while a four-foot-six kid who wasn't going to play in the game anyway was all suited up just to shoot around during warm-ups?

SIZE AND EXPECTATIONS

When do we teach people these hard, cruel facts of life? In fact, what did this young coach teach both boys (and the whole team) that day? That winning is the only thing that matters? That responsibility doesn't count for much? That life always favors the naturally gifted? Yet from your own experience, can you say that these lessons are all that false?

These are important questions which merit some serious consideration, but I just threw them in here to illustrate how often we unknowingly and unintentionally pass along our own values to junior highers.

Their perceptions are probably keener than we think. I would like this incident to lie in the backs of our minds and haunt us a bit every time we make a quick decision or take an action affecting a learning, growing, changing young person.

Whether we agree with this coach's actions or not, we need to look at a couple of the basic factors at work here and see what we can learn from them.

The obvious difference between Kenneth and Chad was size. A foot and a half difference may be a little extreme; but size differences are common at this age. Not only are there differences between individuals, but any one person may encounter a serious size change in what seems like a matter of days.

Chad had probably grown six inches over the summer, and Kenneth would be likely to grow six inches the next summer. Pity the poor mothers and fathers who are trying to keep these guys in clothes, particularly if they are the kind of kids who are always concerned about how they look.

Adults can't do much about the contrast in size of junior highers. But we are able to control our expectations of the junior highers we know. Chad was big, but irresponsible. Kenneth was short, dependable, and unusually mature. Yet they were both thirteen years old. Imagine them side by side. Can you honestly say that you would be capable of treating them as equals? If the two of them showed up to do some yard work for you, could you pay them the same amount without any misgivings? Can you blame the coach for thinking that Kenneth wasn't "big enough" to care about the coach's decision?

This is one of the most serious challenges for people who live or work with junior highers: accepting the fact that young people do not mature in all aspects of his character on the same schedule, and realizing that physical maturity is often deceptive.

ASSESSING MATURITY

There is actually injustice here on both sides. In most people's eyes, Kenneth is still a child. Unless he develops physically, he will be treated as a child for the next two years. We give him the responsibility of a child and we expect him to act like a child, ignoring his potential and maturity.

Chad, on the other hand, is not only saddled with all that size, but is also burdened with people's greater expectations.

They expect him to perform with more maturity than he actually has at this point. Age is no factor here. The bigger a person is, the more is expected of him.

Chad simply does not have the intellectual or emotional maturity to handle the adult responsibility demanded of him. He, like Kenneth, still has a natural need to punch, pester, choke, squeak, slouch, stumble, belch, drop, and forget. He gets just as excited about a new hair on his chest and just as upset about a new pimple on his nose. Even if he has just scored twenty-five points in the basketball game, he still may trip over a line and fall on his face going back to the dressing room. At such times we need to remember that he is just another thirteen-year-old boy.

If you are going to be effective as a parent, you have to develop some method other than size and physical development to assess maturity. Thirteen-year-olds are thirteen years old regardless of how often they shave. This is one of the most difficult problems of the whole junior high scene. It is difficult for all the Chads and Kenneths (and Charlottes and Kristines), and it is difficult for the people who have to work with them.

GOOD LOOKS, BAD TIMING

I remember the first time I ever saw Jessica. I was eating lunch in the school cafeteria, discussing with some other junior high teachers such high-level issues as nuclear disarmament and why the Cowboys never win the Super Bowl. Suddenly, right in the midst of all this profoundness, the conversation stopped. I looked up from my food to see what had shocked us into a state of silence (an unusual condition even at the teacher's table in a junior high lunchroom), and I saw Jessica standing in line.

She was strikingly beautiful, and I began to fumble in my mind with who she might be—an especially mature high school student visiting our building, a student teacher from a nearby college, or perhaps a young mother. The principal, probably anticipating our questions, said, "That's Jessica, the new seventh grader who transferred here this morning."

We sat shocked. As junior high teachers, we had come to expect size and maturity differences in young people, but Jessica was the most extreme example we had ever seen.

As we became acquainted with her in class, we discovered that she had the personality, intelligence, and talent to match her beauty. She was simply a graceful person. Although she was not much sharper than the average seventh grader, she had a certain confidence about herself that carried over into her academic work. She also was cheerful and cooperative.

Because she was so mature physically, the other teachers and I expected her to be more mature in other ways. If she had not completed an assignment on time, we would have been more likely to accept her excuse than if she had looked like any other seventh grader. I don't tell an adult, "Eat your liver before you can have dessert," and I don't think I would have told that to Jessica either.

As the new kid on the block, Jessica was not as enthusiastically accepted by her classmates as she was by the teachers. The in-group (usually a well-established clique) didn't want her. She was too mature and too pretty. She would have had to come into the group as the leader, and the present leadership didn't want that. So she stayed outside.

The out-group is usually easier to get into. Since these people are a little lonely anyway, they welcome new members, so they adopted Jessica. But she didn't fit in there either.

At this point, she wasn't angry with the system. She was still worried about her studies and grades, and pleasing teachers and parents. Although she was gracious and bright enough not to offend anybody, she was never really comfortable with the people who were willing to accept her. Consequently, she spent the seventh grade being more popular with adults than with the people her own age. That was fine with the adults. We all enjoyed her friendship.

However, near the end of the year, Jessica revealed her true value system and made an emphatic statement about what she wanted in life. She wanted to be a typical, popular junior high girl—in other words, a cheerleader. She wanted to wave the pom-poms, chew bubble gum, and yell for the football team.

When tryouts came, she was one of the first to sign up. At our school, cheerleader tryouts were one of the major rites of the year. Each new, hopeful group tried with ever-increasing optimism to outdo everything that had ever been done before.

On the appointed day, the student body marched into the gym to the accompaniment of the band's playing the "Washington Post March." With giggling sincerity, the out-going captain made her farewell speech, a rousing plea for school spirit. Then, participating in pairs, the aspirants led the student body in a cheer as they demonstrated their talents at hollering and waving at the same time. Although Jessica looked a bit out of place because she was about a foot taller than her partner, she was, nevertheless, graceful through the whole ordeal. But when the students cast their secret ballots at the end of the ritual, Jessica didn't make it. She wasn't even close enough to be an alternate.

During the summer, I heard that Jessica was modeling for a local store. When school started the next fall, she was going steady with a high school junior who owned a nice car and a questionable reputation. After that, she only went through the motions of being in junior high. By the time she was seventeen, she had become actively involved in the drug culture, dropped out of school, and moved in with a man several years older than she was. I'm not sure where she is or what she is doing now.

WHEN BEAUTY COMES EARLY

I realize that Jessica is a bit of an unusual case. She was not only mature, but also beautiful at thirteen. Yet she still represents a troublesome group—the junior high girls who mature physically before they do emotionally and intellectually. Jessica made a strong effort to fit into her own age-group, but at that point in a person's development, the age-group is rather narrowly defined. In adulthood, there isn't that much difference between the thirties and the fifties. In high schools, sophomores are frequently comfortable with seniors. But in the stage of early adolescence, seventh graders are seventh graders, and eighth graders are eighth graders.

When Jessica couldn't find her niche among her own age-group, she had to experiment and look outside. She knew she wasn't an adult, so she settled for the next step up—the high schoolers. Maybe she could find some companionship there.

As soon as she paid her dues into that group, she was suddenly thrust into decisions she wasn't prepared to make. Jessica was not experienced enough nor emotionally mature enough to make rational decisions about how to handle drugs or her own sexuality. But because of the way she looked, these decisions were forced on her at a time when peer acceptance was about her only basis for value judgments. It is difficult for anyone to try to live her life on the basis of what she thinks other people want her to do. Small wonder that Jessica became confused, disenchanted, and eventually hardened.

Jessica also teaches us another important lesson. Her story points out the vast difference between thirteen year olds and sixteen year olds. Sometimes those differences may not be immediately obvious. Thirteen year olds may look older, and they may even sound older. Some seventh graders can read, write, and talk as intelligently as many high school juniors. But those three to five extra years of studying at the University of Life have a tremendous value.

Jessica was a normal, sweet, girl who had the body of a woman. The people she encountered were more aware of (and more interested in) the woman than the girl. And we adults who should have known better unwittingly cheated her out of three critical years of development.

What could have been done to prevent Jessica's unhappiness and subsequent disillusionment? The answer to that is more difficult than I would like it to be. We could have told Jessica that being a cheerleader was not all that important, but I don't think she would have believed us. We could have tried to be closer to her ourselves, but she didn't want adult friendship. She already had that. What she wanted was to be a seventh grader among seventh graders. But it is not easy for parents or teachers to manipulate a group of seventh and eighth graders into accepting someone.

If you have a daughter who is maturing physically more rapidly than in other areas, I offer Jessica's story just as it stands. Your daughter may look like she is past this stage, but she is still a junior higher with all the trappings thereof. Your understanding, concern, and sensitivity are crucial.

WHEN BEAUTY FADES EARLY

But what if you have just the opposite problem? What if your daughter's beauty fades earlier than all her friends'? In that case, consider Sara's example.

Sara's teacher was trying to help the seventh grade class understand the concept of romanticism—the idea that something in the distance looks good, but in reality isn't as much fun as you thought it was going to be. The concept was important to their under-standing a short story about Southerners preparing for the Civil War.

To make the experience as personal as possible, the teacher asked, "Have any of you really looked forward to some event and then, when it came, you were totally disappointed by how it turned out?"

Sara's answer was terse and spontaneous. "Yeah. Junior high."

Sara wasn't just having a bad day. Her appraisal was accurate and permanent. So far, her seven months in junior high had been totally disappointing, and things weren't getting any better.

Sara had the flip side of Jessica's problem. Sara had been in school with many of her classmates since they started kindergarten. Very early, she had become a favorite of students and teachers alike. She was pretty and cheerful. She had a nice smile and a big heart. Her classmates loved and envied her at the same time.

She was a good student and had a quick wit, so with her combination of cute and neat, she was also the teacher's pet. But her classmates didn't resent her because she was so friendly.

As the students edged to the upper end of childhood and began to notice that the world was wonderfully coeducational in structure, Sara mastered the art of flirting.

She spread her smiles over a wide enough area to accumulate several male interests, and at the same time she remained popular with the girls. Throughout elementary school, Sara was the center of attention.

But during the summer between sixth and seventh grades, when people are supposed to mature and change, a strange thing happened. Instead of growing tall and feminine as her friends did, Sara only added a few pounds to her already short stature (and in places not necessarily conducive to feminine charm).

When the students reconvened at the junior high in the fall to "ooh" and "aah" at how much everybody had changed over the summer, Sara soon began to lose her center-ring attraction. To make matters worse, she was replaced by her best friend. Although no one intended to be rude to Sara, it was just that the other girl suddenly looked like more fun, and people that age usually trust their eyes.

Sara had enough class not to make any scenes, but she quietly went about trying to reclaim some of the distinction she had lost. She became the first girl in class to wear eye makeup and, after intense pleading with her parents for two weeks, she got her ears pierced. Yet despite all her attempts at cosmetic improvement, things didn't change much. Her best friend was still the center of attention, both with the boys and the girls, and Sara was cast into a supporting role.

Such a change in status never comes easily, particularly when a person has enjoyed stardom as long as Sara had. And it was more painful because the change in roles was dictated by something as superficial as change in body style. Deep down inside, Sara was the same sweet, lovable person she had always been. But suddenly she didn't look as good as her friend on the outside. Why should she be penalized for that?

Sara's struggle, however, was real and deep and far too typical. Of course, it was tough on her, but Sara was a strong enough person to live through her junior high misery. She cried a lot; she was frequently sullen and moody; she spent a lot of time locked up in her room; and she bounced between hatred and loyalty for her classmates. But she survived.

In fact, by her junior year in high school she had managed to reclaim some of the popularity she had lost, and she finished high school on a rather positive note. Now that she is an adult, she has chosen to forget about junior high altogether, to block out of her mind all those unhappy memories of that period of transition.

WHAT'S A PARENT TO DO?

If Sara had been a little less strong, her change in roles could have been devastating. In fact, I chose Sara to illustrate this point because her story does end happily. None of us is happy when our children are unhappy, and any good parent will search for some remedy that will work. Unfortunately, Sara's parents were almost powerless to help. Her problem was something she had to go through alone.

So whether your child, like Jessica, matures early and has to endure the pressure that is involved, or is more like Sara, whose beauty (and popularity) came and went before entering junior high, here are a couple of suggestions to help you see her through those hard times:

First, if your child is nearing that age when body styles and appearance change rapidly, you may as well prepare yourself to suffer with her through some changes in social roles that come with the package. You can't speed up the transition or change the course of it, but you can provide some understanding and perhaps some diversion.

Second, perhaps the best help a parent can offer in similar situations is to help the junior higher see beyond the present. Of course, this is tough for any of us. But if life really becomes miserable for everybody, it might be worth a try. Spend some time with your child reflecting about what life is going to be. Talk of adult things such as work, marriage, and family. Give her some adultlike responsibility.

If you promise not to tell, I'll share my secret weapon, which I save for my children when they are struggling through these critical periods of reidentification. I find a vacant parking lot somewhere, and I teach them how to drive. You would be amazed at how much thirty minutes at the wheel in an isolated parking lot can do for a thirteen year old's morale!

It doesn't resolve the problem. They don't become any more socially accepted, although they may brag about their driving skills all over school. But they have been given a glimpse of what life is going to be like once they get past their immediate obstacles, and that seems to help.

REJECTED!

The teacher's instructions were given in all innocence: "Johnny, think of an adjective and use it in a sentence showing its three degrees."

But Johnny has been waiting all period for this opportunity. He quickly responds: "Robert is *fat*. Robert is *fatter* than anyone I have ever seen. Robert is the *fattest* person in the whole world."

"And the laziest," adds Charles.

"And the ugliest, yech!" adds Marie.

"You would be fat too if you ate like he does," adds another classmate.

Poor Robert . . . and this is still the first hour. Before the day is over, he will be kicked and punched, his sandwich will be squashed, someone will break his pencil, and he will be pushed off the sidewalk while trying to walk home with some of the guys.

Robert represents one of the most difficult challenges for a junior high teacher and even more so for a parent. Junior highers can be very understanding and loving— even tender, on rare occasions. But other times they can be brutally cruel, and usually their cruelty is directed toward one person—in this case, Robert.

ROBERT SERVES A PURPOSE

I am not sure I know how Robert got the office of human football. In some ways he isn't quite as mature as the other students, but he is not that different. Sometimes he may not be so easy to be around, but many other students are just as capable of childish behavior. Yet for some reason, Robert has been designated as everyone else's morale booster. One way to join the "in group" or prove oneself to be a thinking human being is to put Robert down. To achieve this end, almost anything is acceptable.

I don't know how Robert got "elected," but I do think I understand the need for the office. I don't approve, but I understand. It seems to me that there is an innate human need for each one of us to feel that we are better than someone else. This attitude may not be scripturally sound, but it seems to be fairly universal.

For the junior highers, this need seems to be particularly acute. Since they are in the process of change, they really don't know themselves very well. Many are at that awkward age of being too old to be cute and too young to be handsome or beautiful. They are beginning to identify some adult powers (such as reproduction), yet society tells them they shouldn't use these powers. In the midst of all these inconsistencies and contradictions, the junior highers need to reassure themselves that they are all right. They do so by suggesting that Robert isn't. (Adults seem to have the same need to feel superior, though their methods are usually more polite and sophisticated.)

What can we do for Robert? To a teacher, Robert presents an almost unsolvable problem. The English teacher could have stopped that in-class teasing. Had she been forceful enough, she could have made sure that it never occurred in English class again. But she could not have made Robert a popular hero, and the students would have just found another setting in which to persecute him. Besides, by punishing the students for their teasing, she might have actually made matters worse for Robert when class was over.

She might have tried to make Robert better liked, treating the cause and not just the result. But such efforts must be very subtle, lest the students see through them and add one more reason to their mental lists of how to tease Robert. I suggest that Robert's problem needs to be addressed by his parents rather than his teachers.

If Robert is your child, you are going to spend some distressing days before the two of you escape the junior high years. Robert is going to be unhappy, and I am not sure you can prevent that. You might begin by helping him work on his social skills.

Sometimes people need to learn how to take a joke. Or you might try to channel him into a friendship with someone who will accept him. Or, if the situation is really critical, you may want to give Robert some adultlike experiences or responsibilities that will provide some confidence in himself. These efforts may help, but we can't expect miracles. Once a person gets burdened with Robert's role, it is difficult to break free.

On the other hand, if your child is not like Robert, keep in mind that there probably is a Robert at school. You may want to talk to your junior higher about the problems people like Robert face. The best thing that could happen in this situation would be for one popular person to take Robert's side. If the right junior higher accepted him, it could turn the whole process around. So you may want to talk to your child about his work as a junior high minister witnessing to the divine nature of every creature.

A PERSONAL EXAMPLE

It's up to you to initiate a discussion with your teenager. No one likes to bring up the topic of his or her own rejection. I know my children don't. I discovered this at one of our family discussions which take place on occasional days when we "debrief" during dinner. Doesn't that evoke a nice image? My friendly, happy family sitting around the table, leisurely remembering the events of the day, sharing prayer concerns, stopping occasionally to read a relevant passage from Scripture?

Well, it is a nice scene, and at our house we do it regularly. (Notice I said regularly instead of often. To be honest, we take this opportunity about once a month—whether we need it or not. We have this kind of meal whenever no one has to run off for piano lessons, is late getting home from track practice, or has to get to church for a deacons' meeting.)

"Kris," I asked our seventh grader during one of these events, "when are you going to hear the results of the musical tryouts?"

"She posted them today."

"Oh?" (With junior highers, you have to use the art of "encouraging listening.")

"Yeah. Dianne got the part."

After some silence, I replied, "Well, Dianne will do a good job."

"Yeah. She can sing better than me."

After some meager attempts to relieve the tension I had created, I suddenly thought of something more positive.

"How's basketball practice?" That ought to change the tone, I thought.

"Coach called us in today and said that she would only be able to keep twelve girls."

"Oh?" More encouraging listening.

"I wasn't one of the twelve."

At that moment, I was sorry I didn't have a deacons' meeting to rush off to.

Yet, this was a noteworthy night in our family history. Kris had suffered two major setbacks, both in the same day. Despite her lackadaisical attitude and her apparent reluctance to talk about them, she had to be suffering emotionally.

At that point, parents—even those who felt awkward and useless—were valuable to her. Her setbacks provided us not only a challenge but also an opportunity. Here are some things we learned:

1. We had to help our child manage her hurt.

To adults who worry about "important"

things, not getting into a musical may not seem too shattering. But for a seventh grader, it may represent the loss of all the potential joy in the world. There was no doubt about it. Kris was hurt, and we had to help her manage it.

My first impulse when things happen to my children (or to yours, for that matter) is to try to heal the hurt—to kiss it and make the pain go away. That's what I would really like to do, but I know that I can't.

Kris had suffered some setbacks, and she was going to feel some pain. There wasn't a whole lot I could do to make the hurt go away. And I am not sure that would have been the best thing, even if I could. The natural process of growing inevitably leads to a certain amount of suffering, and that suffering is valuable in helping us become mature.

2. We had to help her preserve her pioneering spirit.

Kris had just tackled two challenges. In good faith and with a positive outlook, she had tried to reach into the unknown, to attempt something she had never attempted before. Just trying out for the team and the musical took courage, but both of the challenges had backfired in her face. Her experimental courage had led only to the pain of rejection.

A normal reaction for someone in Kris's position would be to think to herself, *Oh, well, what's the use? I tried and failed. I won't even bother trying the next time.*

But this is a dangerous attitude, particularly for a seventh grader, and presents one of the greatest challenges to parents. Junior highers have to experiment. That is one of the characteristics of the age. But during experimentation, there are always as many setbacks as successes. Somehow, we have to help our children look objectively at their failures and maintain enough confidence to keep trying.

3. We didn't burden Kris with unfair expectations.

The one prayer I pray most frequently as a parent (and a teacher) is that the Lord will give me the wisdom to know how much to expect of my children. If I expect too little of them, they may waste their creative gifts. If I expect too much of them, I may destroy them with an unrealistic burden.

Kris's suffering also caused us pain. We had looked forward to seeing her in the musical, and we had planned to attend the basketball games. But during her crisis, we had to accept our truth and help Kris accept hers.

4. We had to help Kris get her life back in perspective.

That night our after-dinner conversation hit on several stories—some from Scripture, some about great heroes, and some about real-life people we knew. We wondered how Zechariah must have handled the suffering of not being able to speak until his child, John the Baptist, was born. We tried to imagine the drive that possessed Glen Cunningham to recover from serious burns and injury to become a world-class runner. We prayed for a young All-American athlete, a friend of the family, who had just learned that because of a latent back injury, he would never be able to compete in gymnastics again.

These memories weren't meant to divert Kris's attention from her own hurts. We retold these stories to remind ourselves that we are never the only people suffering. We used the examples to gain the courage to accept the fact that life is more than speaking and burn scars and gymnastics honors and junior high musicals and basketball. When we have courageous confidence in the truth of the Gospel, life always has hope.

I don't know if Kris learned all that in one night. But at least there weren't any tear stains on her pillow the next morning.

CASTES AND OUTCASTS

One of the best ways to learn about any wild beast is to study the pack with which it associates. This is particularly true with junior highers, because the grouping is very important to them.

Most junior highers spend a good part of their time and mental energy trying to achieve and maintain some kind of status within a specific social group. Their efforts reveal that it is important to them to belong. Therefore, a study of how any one junior higher behaves and responds will require some analysis of the group that is setting the standards for his thinking, behavior, and appearance.

With some caution about the dangers of generalization, we can classify most junior highers into one of four groups: the Jocks, the Brains, the Regulars, and the Burnouts.

THE JOCKS

Although in its literal sense the term *Jocks* refers specifically to athletes, in actual operation it has a broader definition. The group usually identified by this term consists not only of the athletes and cheerleaders, but also the students who actively support school activities. (Another title for these people is *socialites*.)

This group is everywhere and into everything. They play sports, lead cheers, print the newspaper, play in the band, get parts in the play, make friends with the teachers, and win all the awards at the annual assembly. They are also active outside school. They are officers in the church youth group; they volunteer for local ministries; they are the leaders in scouts and other community groups.

They try to find happiness in being productive, active, and cooperative—working within the system rather than fighting against it. Although they encounter the usual frustrations and setbacks, they are basically satisfied with the general quality of life.

They tend to worry about how they look and what adults think about them, so they keep themselves clean according to junior high standards and try to make the best grades they can without earning the label of being scholarly.

In most schools, this is an old, established group. These people have been friends before, so it seems natural for them to stay together during junior high. Although these sweet, innocent children would never intentionally hurt anybody, the group tends to be closed to outsiders. Once this group is established, it's difficult for anyone to break in.

The exclusiveness of the Jock Club may present one of the cruelest structures of junior high life. How often I have stayed awake at night and prayed for some poor child who wants to be friends with a cheerleader who is already so popular that she doesn't have time for any more friends! It's not that the cheerleader wants to be cruel—but her tight schedule and limited friendship circle have become the cruelest form of rejection for people who need her attention.

The situation is not quite as rigid for boys as it is for girls. For one thing, boys usually have more opportunities to achieve status than girls do. Any boy who participates in sports can usually make it into this club if he wants, and he might actually rise to a position of leadership just because of his athletic activity.

Although there is a need for experimentation, chance, and risk among the Jocks, the members of this group are usually not as defiant as those of the other groups. They may operate on the fringe of structured rules and procedures, but they aren't really trying to destroy the system or live outside it. After all, the system has provided them with the rewards that help them identify themselves, so they want the structure to prevail—even if they have to test it once in a while.

THE BRAINS

I use the label *Brains* to classify a rather select group of junior highers who aren't ashamed to appear intellectual. Although the club isn't sexually exclusive, it tends to be male-dominated.

In many ways the members of this group look and act like normal junior highers (whatever that means). They have growth spurts, voice changes, and skin problems. Like their contemporaries, they fluctuate between childhood and middle age in behavior, attitudes, and interests.

But the Brains differ from the Jocks

because they don't have time for all those childish activities such as basketball and cheering. They are simply too busy with chess, poetry, computers, science fiction, intricate science fair projects, or some other intellectual endeavor.

Since this group is smaller than the Jocks, its members tend to build close friendships with each other. If they are unhappy about not being in the popular group, they rarely mention it. On the other hand, members of this crowd may establish some friendships with adults who have similar interests.

Perhaps the most unusual characteristic about the Brains is that they may not make the best grades. Many leave grade success to the Jocks who need the attention, and settle for applying themselves to their private interests.

I once met a junior high girl who had just published a book of poetry. It wasn't quite *Letters from the Portuguese,* but it was still worth reading on a rainy Saturday. Yet when I stopped by her classroom to congratulate her, I had to wait my turn. A teacher was reminding the young author that she was going to earn a D in English for the semester.

THE REGULARS

In the junior high caste system, the *Regulars* are the equivalent of what politicians once called the silent majority. These people go through life, at least the junior high part of it, without attracting much attention. This is not to say that they don't have their problems. They have as many growth and adjustment struggles as the most active and popular Jock, but since they themselves aren't really big deals to anyone, their problems don't seem like big deals either.

It isn't so much that anyone dislikes them—it's just that no one pays a lot of attention to them. In a typical class situation, the teacher may give as much as eighty percent of his positive reinforcement to the five Jocks, eighty percent of his negative reinforcement to the five Burnouts, and forget the twenty Regulars altogether.

Although they don't distinguish themselves with any great achievements, they don't cause too much trouble, either. They lack the aggressiveness or the confidence necessary to make themselves distinctive in the minds of the people who have the ability to make them important— and most of them don't seem to be too dissatisfied with their lot in life.

The problem is that the standard used to classify a junior higher as a Regular is unrealistic and temporary. Whatever the reasons she is left out of the in-group, these reasons may change during this period of transition. And when these changes occur, the Regular needs to have enough confidence in herself to utilize her talents.

If your child gets cut from the seventh-grade basketball team and thus misses his right to be a Jock, you need to encourage him to keep practicing and to keep trying for the next several years. He may grow and mature and be the best high school basketball player in the class. But we won't know that if he lets his early setback destroy him.

Parents must be alert to the danger: Being a Regular can be a self-fulfilling prophecy. If a student learns in junior high that he isn't mature enough to participate in various activities, he may decide never to try again, even after he matures.

Grades can also become self-fulfilling prophecies. Too often students who make C's decide that they are "C people" and go through life expecting C rewards and C opportunities. As parents who love these people for what they are at the moment they come to us, we can't let this kind of categorization internalize within these junior highers. We need to keep encouraging and recognizing the Regulars for what they can contribute.

This warning is particularly appropriate if your junior higher happens to be a middle child or the second child of the same sex. Since we as parents have been through this before, it is difficult to get as excited about it the next time through. Quite unintentionally we may fail to give the second child as much attention, encouragement, or opportunity as the first one got. And the Regular, if he gets dissatisfied with his inconspicuous role, may try to achieve some attention by moving into the world of the *Burnouts*.

THE BURNOUTS

These are the junior high people who have already had so many setbacks and frustrations that they have just decided not to cooperate with the established system anymore. Their protest ranges from overwhelming lethargy to open and hostile rebellion against all structure and authority.

It is difficult to pinpoint the reasons why a young person would make a decision to quit trying to get attention and feelings of self-worth through the system. Perhaps he has a weakness in some learning skill such as reading, or perhaps he is not as good an athlete, or perhaps he is trying to follow the example of some older people, or perhaps he simply prefers this over the more energetic approach to life.

The unfortunate aspect of the junior high Burnout crowd is that many of them are destined to stay there. There are simply not as many options for fourteen year olds who have chosen not to participate in the established structure. Once they have made that decision, it is difficult for them to change direction.

For one thing, they get so far behind academically that it is almost impossible for them to catch up. Based on their junior high records, they will be directed into high school classes designed for them and will have fewer opportunities to interact with people outside their group.

If a person doesn't succeed at an activity, after a while he loses interest and quits trying. Eventually he seeks success or at least identification in an alternate activity. If your child meets only constant failure or frustration in class, in school activities, in the church group, or even as your child, he will soon quit trying those activities and search for alternatives.

Somewhere there are people who will accept him for who he is and will provide the companionship and understanding he needs. Somewhere there are people who will convince him that success isn't really that big a deal anyhow and that it's all right not to try. Actually, the group bonding may be stronger for Burnouts than for others. Since no one else accepts them, they accept each other.

The school setting is only a frame of reference. For the most part, junior highers stay in their groups wherever they are. Jocks are Jocks wherever you meet them. Though a Regular may get a shot a leadership in, say, a church setting if there are no Jocks around, he is still a Regular for most of the time. Most junior highers internalize their roles in the caste system, and will begin to think of themselves in those roles.

BE WARNED

I present this discussion with all sorts of warnings on the package. Labeling has to be the cruelest of human inventions. I don't think that at creation God said, "I think I will make a Jock this time."

Your child is a unique person who merits your special attention. But at the same time, he does function within the boundaries of a particular social group. If you want to provide your junior higher with some comforting and liberating understanding, you will need to understand something about the characteristics of the group he is in and the group in which he aspires to be.

HELPING FAMILIES GROW SERIES

❧ *Communicating Spiritual Values Through Christian Music*

❧ *Equipping Your Child for Spiritual Warfare*

❧ *Family Vacations that Work*

❧ *Helping Your Child Stand Up to Peer Pressure*

❧ *How to Discover Your Child's Unique Gifts*

❧ *How to Work With Your Child's Teachers*

❧ *Helping Your Child Love to Read*

❧ *Improving Your Child's Self-Image*

❧ *Preparing for Your New Baby*

❧ *Should My Child Listen to Rock Music?*

❧ *Spiritual Growth Begins At Home*

❧ *Surviving the Terrible Teenage Years*

ABOUT THE AUTHOR

Dr. Cliff Schimmels knows the struggles teens face during the adolescent years. He has been a teacher, coach, principal, pastor, newspaper editor, and a professor of education at Wheaton College in Wheaton, Illinois. He is currently using his teaching skills on a two-year assignment in the Soviet Union.

Cliff has written an entire series on how you as a parent can help your child get the most out of school. His *School Success Series* includes:
• *It's Time For School*
• *How to Shape Your Child's Education*
• *What Parents Try to Forget About Adolescence*
• *Notes from the World's Oldest Freshman*
• *How to Survive and Thrive in College*